How to Help Someone with Depression

An Essential Guide for Understanding, Living with, and Helping to Support Someone with Depression

by Rafe Uribe

Table of Contents

Introduction

One of the largest ticking time bombs in 21st century healthcare isn't Ebola or Swine Flu. Nor is it AIDS or STDs. In fact, the drastically rising drug abuse and alcoholism trends should be ample symptomatic information to deduce the answer: **it's depression**. What starts off as anxiety or stress - when left unresolved - can easily develop into clinical depression, a term encountered far more often today than at any other point in the history of human civilization. Approximately 1 in 10 Americans face depression in their lives at one point or another, and 80% of these individuals don't receive any help for it. Moreover, the number of "depression" diagnoses increase by roughly 20% each year.

Whether it's because of an unfulfilling life, rising responsibilities, difficulties in making one's mark in the world, the hypocrisy of virtual social connections leading to the inability to make real or meaningful ones, or just simply increasing dissatisfaction with life in general in an era where the freedom of choice has promised utopian living: There are innumerable reasons for depression, from purely physiological imbalances to complex existential envy. However, the true horror of depression lies in its ability to not only torment its victims, but also the people around them.

Because depression makes it impossible for its victims to *feel* deep-seated emotional attachments even where they genuinely exist, helping them becomes that much more difficult. Furthermore, in attempting to help the victims of depression, people often ignore the psychological toll on themselves until it's too late. Which then simply leads to dissatisfaction, bringing another person to the doorstep of depression, thus further compounding the original victim's psychological turmoil, and so the cycle continues round and round in a vicious dance of destruction and anguish, tainting every person with whom it comes into contact.

Therefore, rather than teaching depression victims to drag themselves out of this mindset—which is more improbable as an accomplishment—it's become far more important to educate people around them to help themselves and the victims together. And that's the reason behind this guide. So, compiled within this book lies decades-worth of experience, aimed at helping you help yourself and your loved one going through this insidious disorder. First Lesson: No, it's not a voluntary choice for them to suffer, which means they can't simply choose to just "snap out" of it. Ready for Lesson Two? Then, let's get started!

5

6

Chapter 1: Understanding Depression

Though there have been several pop culture representations of depression, they're often blown way out of proportion or given an unduly slanted idea of this disorder for the sake of effective dramaticism. Not every depression victim thinks of suicide right away, but if the disorder takes enough of a hold—that's where it eventually ends up. But what if you could catch this at a much earlier stage, when the victim has just started sliding into its clutches? There are several forms and magnitudes in which depression hits its victims, and the first thing which you need to understand is the complete picture of the manifestation of depression.

Often, the first major symptom is drastic changes in mood, sleeping, and eating patterns. Depression—regardless of origin or cause—often reflects a change in the neurochemistry of the victim. Whether the changes or depression itself comes first is rather like wondering whether the egg came before the chicken. What *is* known is that three neurotransmitters are often affected—serotonin, norepinephrine, and dopamine. These chemicals dictate many things in the human brain directly and indirectly, from appetite to libido, from perception of joy to outlook on life, from pain thresholds in the body to energy levels, etc. Now, the purpose of informing you of this chemical aspect of depression is to make you understand that this feeling doesn't just exist in the heads of victims. It has a physical basis, and a recognizable change in body chemistry. Whether an imbalance in neurotransmitters caused the depression, or the other way round, the way your loved one feels about himself/herself is quite real.

Mood changes are often accompanied by a radical diminution in positivity and a growth towards negative or unfavorable outlooks. It may also lead to isolation and seclusion from normal bonds in their lives, like close friends and family. However, since this also sounds like normal teenagehood in many aspects, there are secondary symptoms to watch out for as well. The occurrence of depression is often accompanied by major changes in eating and sleeping patterns. Where someone would eat very little before, they now engorge themselves with food all the time, or vice versa. If they slept very little or as much as needed before, they prefer lazing around and sleeping in their own space over any other activity.

Depression also marks severe changes in libido, as a person loses much or all of their sexual interest and drive. Again, this isn't just psychological, nor is it personal. If you're their partner, you could be the hottest person in the world to them and yet there would be no response. It's not because they don't feel for you or aren't attracted to you. But, with how miserable they feel, sexual thoughts are literally the last things on their minds. Again, another clarification needed here for partners is that sex lives don't lead to depression. Failing or diminishing sex lives are a symptom of depression, not a cause.

Victims with depression lose energy, drive, and ambition rather quickly. Where they may have been powerhouses before, now even the smallest efforts leave them winded and tired. Moreover, even if they continue to follow their duties or responsibilities, they now do so with an air of being burned out, and only perform the minimum required of them by their standards. They're also less decisive than before, and may seek to push even the smaller decisions onto the shoulders of others.

Though they may still continue along the same personal, academic, or professional path as before, they may seem less driven than they were about reaching their end goal. This is also why it's quite common for victims of depression to veer severely off path when they suffer through this disorder— often negating months or years worth of hard work and advancement with their behavior, or choosing to wile away their time instead of doing anything productive. It's not because they don't care about their efforts or those of others, but they literally can't feel the concern they once held anymore, or even understand why it mattered so much to them anyway.

Regardless of how close you may have been to the victim before their bout of depression, emotional appeals and attachments again don't bear any fruit in particular. This isn't because they don't care about themselves or about you, but the storm of anguish they usually hide inside themselves often leads to emotional numbness within them. There's so much

10

going on inside their head that it doesn't have space for your added emotions and appeals. Therefore, if they don't react the way you want them to or behave emotionally in a manner which you had seen them previously adhere to, it's because adding any more emotions within that turmoil just isn't possible for them. Nevertheless, the numbness which we just spoke of isn't always an automatic next step from being so emotionally stimulated within their own heads. Often, people suffering from depression willingly choose that emotional numbness as a defensive mechanism to protect themselves from entirely losing their minds.

This leads us to the next point—alcoholism and drug abuse. This is often seen leading in two different directions, either towards complete surrender to drugs and alcohol, or tee totalitarianism. The first group often consists of people who may or may not have experimented with or imbibed such chemicals before. But, with the emotional turmoil within their heads, and the thought pattern of depression victims which mentally closes all outlets for these emotions, they succumb to drugs and alcohol as a way of artificially keeping their spirits high and combating the emotional storm by chemically numbing it.

The second group usually consists of people who have had a low to heavy involvement with drugs and/or alcohol in their lives, and who may have dealt with depression or other psychological issues in some form or magnitude before. Such people are wary of falling into harmful coping habits, and so retract to complete abstinence from drugs and alcohol to remove all temptation. While both of these groups represent marked changes in behavior towards chemicals and possible addiction, falling into this second group is a good sign for loved ones around them. It means that these people are ready and willing to fight their condition, rather than give in to it.

Regardless of whether they're involved with substance abuse, victims of depression often display extreme mood swings and temper control issues. They may quickly develop an intensely negative outlook on everything in their lives, including themselves and their self-image and worth. They start ignoring whatever good may occur in their lives, whether as a result of others interacting with them or even because of actions they took themselves. This is one of the harshest truths about depression. When talking about depression, people often use phrases like "the colors were sucked out of my life," and this is quite literal not metaphorical. While they still *see* colors, they seem duller in comparison, and the psychological effects of colors on their mentality is entirely subdued and muted, thus often adding to the gloom. This is one of the reasons why depressed people gravitate towards muted colors and dark surroundings—the strange feeling of vibrant colors adding no sense of joy to the visual sense of stimulus gets quite off-putting and adds to the turmoil after a while.

If one is to describe depression in a single word, the closest equivalent would be "quicksand". Depressed people often feel horrendously helpless and trapped, and feel unable to break out of this mentality no matter what they may try. Often this conclusion is reached without actually trying anything positive, because the sapped energy and drive means that they would be more likely to reach this conclusion as a foregone truth—"No matter what I do, I won't feel better. So what's the point of trying?"

Again, this isn't a choice, but a natural escalation of all the various factors which we've discussed so far, which is why it irritates them further when people try to push conversation or ways out on them, culminating in the oft-repeated "You don't understand me," or "How would you possibly know about this better than me, especially when I'm the one going through all this and not you?" These aren't just movie dialogues, but real conversations which people around depression victims often face when they try and help them—which then leads to bitterness and emotional distancing of the person who was genuinely trying to help, but was shut down so abruptly.

As you must be starting to understand, depression often pushes its victims and the people around them into a catch-22. How can you help someone who can't lift a finger to help themselves, because their own mind has them convinced that all efforts are doomed to failure? After all, whether you bring the camel to the water well, or water to the camel, you can't force it to drink it if it doesn't want to. Furthermore, if everything you read in this chapter about the emotional state of someone battling depression left you even slightly overwhelmed, can you imagine actually going through this? This isn't the equivalent of having a bad day or week, but rather the sensation of every single moment, action, event, and person being against you and your joy in some odd manner, and that every iota of effort you spend is just wasted on a black hole of "Nothing will ever change, and you will never feel better again."

But, there is an answer, and here it is—stop trying to *fix* it, because you can't. What you *can* do is try and elevate it little by little and coax your loved one to get some help. There's a reason why it's called *clinical* depression, in the sense that this particular disorder poses such pathological dangers to the psyche of your loved one that an amateur layman or woman can't hope to solve through some magic exercise or phrase. The only way out is getting the people suffering from it to see some value in their existence, and choose to seek help themselves. That is a definite way in which you *can* help. While depression may come and go in smaller magnitudes, often requiring no help apart from some time alone, leaving sufferers be during this time is extremely risky since it can just as easily descend into much worse states.

Chapter 2: Living with a Victim of Depression

Now, if the previous chapter has helped you identify depression in your loved one for sure, then this chapter is extremely important for you. Because, this won't deal with their issues or problems, but with *yours*—your needs, and ways in which you need to reduce the psychological damage of living with someone suffering from depression.

Here's the problem—in our society, whenever someone suffers from some sort of illness, people around them treat their own joy and happiness as a dirty secret for which they must feel guilty about. Whether it's someone going through a physiological illness or a psychological problem, loved ones around them adopt this mantle of "I shall suffer right alongside you, my own happiness be damned." But why?

I've known several patients with terminal illnesses in my time, and absolutely none of them have wished for their loved ones to be unhappy just because of them. In fact, what they wished for more than ever was to see *more* joy in the lives of loved ones around them, rather than less, because they knew that they wouldn't have the same happy outcomes. They wished for their loved ones' lives to be larger and more spectacular than ever before, and watching all of them sacrifice their own happiness for some silly notion of guilt over the patient's circumstances only added to their own troubles with depression and sorrow.

However, regardless of how often or eloquently I explain this, people always come back with the same response—it's because we're compassionate. But this isn't compassion, it's cowardice that only aggravates the original problem to begin with. If someone else's wedding broke off in disastrous form, not rubbing your own upcoming nuptials in their face is compassion—not being happy about it at all because of some sense of guilt is ridiculous. Moreover, in the case of depression, how exactly are you going to help your loved one feel any better if you end up just as miserable as them?

One reason why people behave this way is because they confuse being together around loved ones with being the same person—especially in the case of partners and parents. They want to bond and synchronize with the other person so deeply that they wish to behave as two parts of the same organism. But that's not the case. It's good that you care about your loved one so much, but you're still two brains and two bodies. If you wouldn't stop eating just to give them company in their depression, why would you stop feeling happy? Your brain and body need to continue along the same track as before if you wish to provide your loved one with a solid foundation from which to pick themselves back up. When professionals don't see fit to treat drug addicts by throwing them in a festering pit of disease and addiction, how exactly would patients with depression be able to recuperate if the entire atmosphere around them were gloomy, sad, heavy, or tense because you aren't looking after your needs either. The treatment to darkness is sunshine, not hiding in the basement under a black quilt with the lights off.

So, even if your loved ones are suffering from depression, don't put your life on hold. It's understandable if you don't wish to leave them alone at home, but that's not necessary. Instead of spending your time in isolation as well, keep calling over small groups of people from both your social circles who are generally upbeat and happy, and who interact well with your loved one on a general basis.

If their depression isn't that bad yet, then *do* spend some time outside recharging your own batteries. During this time, make the switch to healthier foods and rearrange your routine so that you get ample rest and are living a wholesome lifestyle. This would be far better than wracking your brains wondering how to help them while dragging yourself into the same pit which they're trying to escape.

Most importantly, do not let your own life or joys go off track. Keep working or studying hard to achieve your goals, and share your joys with your loved one. While compassion does indeed dictate that you should be tasteful about how you discuss your achievements and successes if your loved one is facing a harsh battle in life, you need to present yourself as a role model for them.

Though patience is certainly called for in great quantities while dealing with people battling depression, don't close yourself off and soak in all the negativity. Ensure that you have at least one trusted person with whom you can share the frustrations and problems faced in your day-to-day life with the victim. If you don't wish to share such details with people who know both of you, seek help from a psychiatrist yourself. The point here isn't you needing a shrink, but that you need to talk to someone else—a journal or diary just won't cut it here. You need human interaction with someone who knows and understands the problems in your situation. In no way will this weaken you as a person, but will instead purge you of your bottled emotions so that you can keep going back into the battle with your loved one's depression without feeling like you've had enough and need to give up.

The way to keep yourself on the strong track so that you can keep your mood up while helping your loved one is to value your individual needs just as much as you take care of theirs. The mistake that people make here is in assuming that such a move would be selfish. However, if your loved one is a strong tree, you're their roots. If the roots shrivel up and die for whatever reason, the tree won't survive either.

Therefore, since you're bravely taking up this battle to help your loved one, make yourself into the strongest support possible to be able to help them stand on their own two feet again.

Chapter 3: How to Support a Sufferer of Depression

As I mentioned in the previous chapter, you will need an incredible amount of patience when dealing with victims of depression. Every self-respecting person has their own personality, opinions, pride, and self-esteem—and these are sorely wounded on a regular basis when dealing with depressed people. Parents and partners of people battling with this disorder often make the mistake of blaming themselves for this condition. Once they're worn down enough, they'll start getting more abrupt or distanced even if they don't understand or recognize this themselves. However, this isn't and has never been your fault. You could have been the absolute perfect parent or partner and this would still have happened, because depression is caused by a convergence of so many varied factors that expert researchers still haven't been able to find the exact cause. Moreover, while you may not recognize the fact that you're slowly distancing yourself from them, in an unconscious bid to protect yourself, I can assure you that the sufferer will recognize it if they have been depending on your support. This will only reaffirm their own low opinion of their life and self-worth.

Moving on, patience isn't the same as humoring odd or hostile behavior, or even walking on eggshells around them. If you do that, you're not helping them. Instead, you're turning into an enabler whose actions lead the depressed person to think that their behavior is justified. You're not being patient with them, but rather pitying them—which will just hurt them in the long run. If you treat them as if the smallest strong action on your behalf would shatter them as if they were made of porcelain, that's precisely how they'll start treating themselves as well. Instead, without being cruel or thoughtless or even lecturing them on being too "easily affected" or "thin-skinned" about everything, you need to impart a quiet and strong air of confidence and composure while dealing with them. You need to find a way to set them right if they start behaving too oddly, without being callous about it.

So, if you ever see behavior which wasn't justified, or if they over-reacted or underwent a mood swing out of nowhere in a manner which was completely out of perspective, mentally retreat to a calm place instead of engaging them on their emotional turf. Then, just speak to them soothingly and warmly, and first remind them that you care for them deeply. After reassuring them several times of your affection for them, just communicate your own feelings of hurt to them in a composed manner, and inform them of your wish to simply help them. It may often happen that this could be met with hostility, sorrow, or any number of negative feelings from them, but don't let them run out or end the conversation. Don't communicate your feelings in a manner or tone that might suggest "Look, I'm trying to help you and see you're treating me badly." Instead, your communication with them is simply to gently hold up a mirror to their actions so they can realize their uncharacteristic behavior towards you.

If a few moments of silence is needed to help them calm down, give them that. If they get angry and vent at you, let them for a while. However, you don't need to leave them alone to give them space—silence can achieve that just as well. Once they seem to have petered out of whichever emotion they directed at you, simply reinforce the same message that you care for them and that they're important to you.

One of the worst things that depressed people undergo is that they lose their sense of self-esteem.

While they may be genuinely angry or upset at the world, or may even feel crushed or defeated by it, their emotions are directed *at the world* and not you specifically. They react in such a manner because they feel lost and alone, and detest that feeling. Therefore, you need to make sure that you keep reinforcing the fact through constant reminders to them that they are *not* alone. You care about them deeply, and you'll help them in any way necessary to battle this disorder. But you will not leave them alone to sulk and wallow.

For example, if they don't wish to eat or come out of the bedroom for breakfast, tell them that you'll make them breakfast in bed but on one condition—you would like to spend at least a little time with them in the morning before you need to get on with your daily schedule as well, and so you want them to accompany you in the kitchen while you prepare the breakfast. And that's non-negotiable, otherwise you'll keep annoying them till they give in. Once breakfast is made, prep some funny show on the TV or a laptop, and leave them to enjoy breakfast in peace. No matter what, you will have succeeded in getting them to step out of their sulk-shell, and have an interaction with you before the day proceeds. Take that as a small but important victory.

As I mentioned in the previous chapter, make sure that you have small groups to accompany you around the victim from time to time. Making sure that the friends of your loved ones as well as your own that are around give the sufferers plenty of opportunities for short interactions. Even if they don't wish to spend every moment of their time with company at home, these small talks will do them loads of good, and will help them keep their heads above water during this battle. Since these would be people who usually interact well with the sufferer, they may also help break through the shell that most depressed people develop around them, and may help in emotional breakthroughs that may provide clues about the origins of the depression.

Finding ways to talk to depressed people is extremely important. By and large, the first thing that happens in depression is a loss of interest in socializing, whether with friends or family. However, keep a depressed person talking for long enough and often enough, and you may gain enough information on how to help them out of it. So, the last thing which you need to do is to help them open up about the way they feel, so that you can start figuring out the root of the problem—relationship, career, studies, whatever it may be. This is particularly important, especially if their life was going well according to them, but they just started feeling bad out of nowhere. This may point to a hormonal imbalance, in the absence of any concrete problems, and can be easily sorted out through medications. But, you'll never know till you find out. This step may need time and a lot of effort for you to get them to open up. Sometimes, you may even need to be shrewd about it, and question about parts of their life which *might* have been the original problem, without being too openly inquisitive about their depression.

However, regardless of whether or not you manage to get any information out of them, you need to find a way to make them understand gently and warmly that they're not well, and that you need to take them to someone who can help. Keep reinforcing their importance in your life and the great values which they themselves possess. If they show the slightest resistance to the prospect, promise to help with every step—even going to the psychiatrist with them if they wish. In cases of depression, it's important that a professional be able to take a look at them before they sink too deeply into it.

Chapter 4: How to Change the Mood

Between taking care of your own needs, and trying to help them get to a psychiatrist, there are plenty of things you can do to make sure that they feel either uplifted little by little, or at least that they are able to keep their heads above water enough to not sink entirely into depression.

One way is to enforce social nights between the two of you. Whether the person going through this is a partner, child, parent, or a friend, you care enough to try and get them out of this quicksand. This means that in some way you have enough access to their life to try and find ways to help. Therefore, the easiest thing you can do is schedule movie nights or some such activities, where you go out once a week and enjoy a film of your choice or theirs.

Though you're sure to meet quite a lot of resistance to this idea, you need to try hard to convince them of it no matter what. If they aren't ready or willing to choose the movies, do your own research and search for comedies and other light-hearted features. If there aren't enough movies to satisfy this need, search for plays or some other such performance activity. The point is to get them out of the house and to enjoy themselves, no matter how briefly it may be.

Another ideal thing to do when getting them out of the house would also be to get them to exercise with you, or go on short walks or jogs. While this may be met with even more resistance, the endorphins released through exercise will help them combat the depression on their own. It's possible that if you manage to convince them to exercise even for a single day, their own perceived uplifted mood would mean that they would resist the idea of continuing this activity with you far less over the next few days. This will also help them improve their self-image in case they've turned into binge eaters because of their depression. Their lagging state of physical fitness in comparison to before will be sure to add to their mental anguish, and will deteriorate their self-confidence and self-worth.

However, the exercises are to help them *feel* fitter, and not shrink to a skeleton—since our self-image is only tied to pounds and kilos when we aren't feeling good about ourselves to begin with. Therefore, if they do start exercising, there's another way to take advantage of their greater interest in food—start experimenting with and exploring new foods and cuisines. If they have taken to food during their depression, take them to a new place whenever you go out for a movie. Try to go to food places which have either newly opened up in town or even ones that the sufferers may have wished to go to before, but never quite got the time or opportunity. This sense of "new" will allow them to step outside their shell, and will give you the opportunity to turn their greater interest in eating into a weapon against the depression which is causing it in the first place.

One last way of keeping moods up, and this is decidedly a strange yet scientifically backed method, is to make sure there's ample contact between them and their family. If you're a parent, make sure that they stay in touch with cousins and other siblings. Or else, you can call up a close friend of theirs, if you see their mood lag, and then hand them the phone to converse for a while. If you're a partner, just call up the parents once in a while if you can, talk for a bit, then hand your loved one the phone. Again—decidedly strange, but effective nonetheless. Make sure that they stay in touch with family and friends throughout this ordeal, because they need as many reminders as possible that they have a bunch of people who care about them, all of whom are rooting for them to feel better.

Chapter 5: How to Change the Atmosphere

Most importantly, you need to brighten up your living environment more so than before. Add bright and soothing paintings or posters up on the walls, change bedsheets, draperies and so on to brighter colors. Change your wardrobe to brighter colored clothing as well. If you have them, but they aren't usually your style—mix it up and wear lighter colors instead for a bit.

Do the same for the sufferer as well, and you should already know that this will be met with a *lot* of resistance. However, surrounding oneself or one's wardrobe entirely with muted, dark, or dull colors when in a depressed state simply adds to it all. Bright and soothing colors have been scientifically proven to exert a lightening effect on the psyche of humans wearing or seeing them—except for red, which induces rage or great passion ("passion" is a tricky concept, since technically anger is a particular form of passion as well). Therefore, keep their residence as bright and cheerful as possible, and do the same to their wardrobe.

Also, add motivational or positive posters wherever you can. They don't need to be extremely cheesy, but they will help your loved one find some base for positive thinking—which can strongly help them battle their depression.

Apart from that, there are several other simple ways of brightening up the atmosphere around the sufferer as well. When you're at home, keep upbeat music playing around the house. Even if your music tastes differ, if your loved ones did listen to any soothing or happy music before their bout with depression, play it loud enough for them to be able to hear it too. While playing music loud enough around the house may not be your usual style, it has a powerful effect on mood. Also, the common denominator of music may provide a basis for more interactions that may help them reduce the severity of their suffering.

Conclusion

Before you do anything, the first thing you need to understand and accept is this—it's not their choice to suffer through this. And yes, I'm quite aware that most people know this. But, in my experience, knowing this fact and *accepting* it aren't quite the same thing—so you need to accept it, and change your vocabulary accordingly when you speak to them.

Even the strongest supporters of sufferers with depression lose their patience sometimes and lash out in ways like "Are you even *trying* to feel better?" or "Nothing that I do helps you." Or even "Why does everything affect you so much? Look at me or Pete or Kat. We've had ups and down too, and this doesn't affect us this much." Unless you've personally dealt with depression in your past, and again this isn't the equivalent of a few bad days, you're really in no position to compare yourself to someone who's suffering through it. I understand that this is difficult to accept, especially among those people who see sufferers and are hell-bent on trying to make them feel better. But it's likely that only 2 out of every 5 things you attempt will have any positive effect whatsoever. It's also likely that many of the changes needed and outlined in this book will require stringent efforts and repeated attempts on your behalf—but you can't give up. The price you would pay for doing so would be too high.

But that's also the reason why you can't do this by yourself. Just as the sufferer will have you as a support, you'll need a supporter to help you recharge, vent, and retain your strength as well—so don't alienate your most trusted friends just because you don't wish to talk about it. Also, the end-game in all of this is to help your loved one understand that they have so much to offer to the world, and so many people love them as they are. Therefore, they need to reach a point of realization where they either admit their problem and try to face it head-on themselves, or they admit to needing help and, with your support and company, start seeing a professional. If possible, and if the depression is bad enough, make sure that the latter scenario comes to pass no matter what. This is important because, in many cases, just talking or undergoing emotional breakthroughs won't be enough, they may need medication to help them feel good enough to try to start their fight back to normalcy. However, with your help, this is a fight they *can* and *have to* win!

Finally, I'd like to thank you for purchasing this book! If you found it helpful, I'd greatly appreciate it if you'd take a moment to leave a review on Amazon. Thank you!

Made in the USA
Monee, IL
14 May 2021